Round Tower Churches
Hidden Treasures of North Norfolk

A series of detailed day tours of the round tower churches of North Norfolk

Foreword by

The Reverend Michael Vockins, O.B.E.

Text and photographs
by Jack Sterry

Acknowledgements

I would like to express my appreciation to family and friends who have helped and encouraged me in the writing of this short book.

As I am one of the dying breed of 'computer illiterates', I am particularly grateful to Pam and Allan Paterson for the great help they have given me with the typing and setting out of the many drafts I have prepared.

To my great friend Mike Vockins, my special thanks for his excellent foreword and encouraging words.

To Rosemary, who has given me warm encouragement and companionship on many of my numerous visits to most of the churches.

To Associated Newspapers Limited, many thanks for their kind help in supporting me towards the sponsorship of this book.

To Mr. W.J. Goode, who I have never met, for the inspiration I first gained from the reading of his great publication, 'Round Towered Churches of South-East England'.

First published 2003

Published by Jack Sterry
Sleepy Hollow 1A De Montfort Road Kenilworth CV8 1DF

ISBN 0-9544948-0-6

Printed & bound by Crowes Complete Print, Norwich

Contents

Foreword

by Rev'd Mike Vockins O.B.E.

Each of us carries in our heart a special place that we love and treasure. Some are lucky to live there permanently, to be truly part of it, and to be coloured by its culture and customs. For others it is a place to which we hastily return whenever we can, sometimes in our imagination and—happy day—sometimes by visiting in person.

Those who read this delightful, charming and stimulating book quickly will become aware of Jack Sterry's deep love of Norfolk. Although Gloucestershire-born he grew up and spent his early life in Norwich. He is ever grateful for the rounded education which the City of Norwich School—and Norfolk itself—provided and, understandably, is immensely proud of having represented his county at sport.

Adult life and the need to earn a living took Jack away from Norfolk, to Leeds, to Ireland and, latterly, to the Midlands. Wherever he has made his home he has contributed to the life of that place, through both its business communities and its sporting communities. It is his nature to do so, for he is a 'giver' and an enthusiast, an enthusiast for so much of what life offers.

That enthusiasm shows itself in many ways, none more marked than the way he remains drawn to his beloved Norfolk. That enthusiasm has been aroused by Norfolk's special (and almost unique) treasures, its round tower churches. Wartime travel restrictions made it difficult, or unwise, to travel far afield and so Jack, as a young Norwich schoolboy, was wholly unaware of these jewels. But by being drawn constantly back to 'his' home county he has discovered new places, new views, new horizons—and round tower churches.

Now in this book he shares his enthusiasm with us, not in the way of an intensely learned expert or an historian who has buried himself (or herself) in the subject for decades, but as someone who is excited by these treasures of Norfolk and who, typically, wants to share his enjoyment. This book will appeal to arm-chair readers (who can mine among the jewel stones) but undoubtedly it is the motorists, the cyclists, the walkers, the ones who want to get out and discover for themselves, who will richly enjoy this work. All will enjoy the photographs too, the fruit of another of Jack's enthusiasms.

As a rural clergyman you would expect me to encourage you to visit country churches, wouldn't you? As one of Jack's fellow sportsmen (and one who has valued his friendship for more than twenty years) you might, perhaps, expect me too to encourage you to get up, go out, and actively follow in Jack's footsteps. I defy you not to be inspired to go and look at these ancient wonders, and I defy you too not to find yourselves drawn into a deeper fascination with Norfolk's round tower churches.

You may find more learned tomes on their history, architecture, and construction; there may be more informative travel guides—but few will give you such a flavour of these delightful places and amazing buildings, or encourage you to share the journeys to pastures new and the joy of discovery Jack Sterry generously and enthusiastically shares with us here. Enjoy your reading, enjoy your searching, and enjoy your own discovering of these wonderful round tower churches.

(Mike Vockins is Hon Curate of three small rural parishes in Herefordshire and Rural Dean of Ledbury. Until 'active semi-retirement' beckoned recently he was, for thirty years, Secretary of Worcestershire County Cricket Club in which capacity he managed four England Under 19 XI and England 'A' team overseas tours. It was in this capacity also that he encouraged Jack Sterry in formulating a national one-day cricket competition for the Second XIs of the First-class Counties, in which a number of recent and current England cricketers made early representative appearances).

Introduction

I grew up during the war years living in Norwich and like many of my age group, spent most of my time kicking or hitting a ball about or making model aircraft to which we added the rather morbid hobby of cycling out to find crashed aircraft. Sadly it was more often one of ours rather than the enemy! We also spent a great deal of our time in air raid shelters, either at home during the night and often at school when we had the risk of daylight raiders, particularly in the early part of the war. This was not the easiest time to obtain one's basic education and I'm afraid mine suffered, hopefully to have been retrieved a little in later years!

Whilst I was a fairly regular churchgoer, I lived in an area of Norwich where there were no round tower churches and I am afraid I must admit that I never even noticed them elsewhere. In fact, until a few years ago I hardly knew of their existence.

Business took me away from Norfolk from my early twenties, although I continued to visit the area, particularly Norwich and north Norfolk quite regularly—mainly the Blakeney and Wells-next-the-Sea areas.

I had always been aware of the very large number of churches in the Norwich district; in fact it was always said that before the war there was "a church for every week and a pub for every day of the year". However times have changed, with many medieval churches particularly in the city being either demolished or put to other usage, I believe partly because of a misguided committee set up shortly after the war.

Luckily because of the work of various strong-minded and tenacious people who decided that this was a frightening proposition, various actions were taken. This was a gradual basis, but in time The Norfolk Churches Trust and other bodies were formed to set out to preserve Norfolk's vast medieval wealth particularly in the country areas. Driving round Norfolk even on the main roads, sometimes if one is on a slight slope, you can see two or maybe three churches within a very small area. Over 650 medieval churches still remain in Norfolk. It is, I understand, one of the, if not the largest collection of medieval buildings in the world in a similar sized area.

But how did I become particularly interested in Round Tower churches? On one of my visits to Norfolk a few years ago, I was driving from Wells-next-the-Sea towards Hunstanton. Away to my left I saw a lovely church set in an excellent position on the hill overlooking the fields, the marshes and ultimately, the sea. This church was St. Margaret's at Burnham Norton, still one of my favourites. As we drove towards Hunstanton, I passed another Round Tower church at Burnham Deepdale and, laid back on the right hand side a little way further along, another church at Titchwell. These rural round tower churches, which I had never even noticed before, attracted me strongly. Their age, their beauty and their very individual character impressed me. I must admit I was 'smitten' and purchased several books and pamphlets including an excellent book entitled "Round Tower Churches of South-East England" written by Mr. W.J. Goode, president of the Round Tower Church Society.

It was interesting to read that there are still some 129 round tower churches today in Norfolk together with the ruins of several others. There are also 42 in Suffolk with a few ruins. Round tower churches are very much an East Anglian phenomena as there are only a few others outside East Anglia namely in Essex, Cambridgeshire, Sussex and Berkshire. Only one other UK region has similar churches and that is in the Shetland and Orkney Islands, where one round tower church still survives. I believe in total there are 180 or so round tower churches still remaining in the United Kingdom.

The history of the churches is interesting and often rather contradictory. There is one area of opinion that maintains that none of the churches are Saxon or Saxo-Norman but were built at rather a later date during, say, 12th to 14th century. From my very limited knowledge, I find this very difficult to accept or understand; Mr. Goode, in his excellent book mentioned above, details in great length the result of his studies over some thirty years or so and feels that maybe 70–75% of the churches, or at least part of them, i.e. the towers or other parts, are at least from the Saxon or early Norman period. In addition it is widely accepted by historians that there are stone built Saxon churches in Yorkshire, Northamptonshire, Herefordshire and Gloucestershire, where local building materials were used—so why not in Norfolk?

There are many theories as to 'why round towers'. Some feel there may have been a Viking influence. In fact the Norfolk County Council are participating in a project investigating the North Sea Viking links between Norfolk and our neighbours in parts of Germany, Scandinavia and Holland who also had strong Viking links. It appears that the Vikings settled extensively in Norfolk and parts of Suffolk toward the end of the 9th century and various Viking objects have been discovered in both counties in recent years. There is a school of thought that an instruction went from a King Athelstan in 937 AD that bell towers should be built. King Athelstan was formerly Guthrum, a Viking leader who led the settlement in the Norfolk area. The dimensions of most of the round towers are fairly precise and it is possible that the instructions from King Athelstan were transmitted via the Saxon cathedral in North Elmham to the outer regions of Norfolk.

Large stone was not easily available in Norfolk or Suffolk so the Saxons used local stones which were predominantly flint, conglomerate, known as pudding stone, and carstone, very much a north-west Norfolk stone known as gingerbread stone. Some historians feel that flint has been mainly used in building the round towers because there were no large corners to cater for. Many of the towers however, also contained blocks or pieces of conglomerate and carstone as well as using all these materials in constructing other parts of the early churches. There is evidence that after the Conquest in 1066 there was a Saxo-Norman overlap where the early Saxon methods were adopted with Norman modifications. After the Conquest the Normans had the benefit of greater technology and the transport facilities for moving larger pieces of stone. They were able to insert dressed stone from other areas of Britain and often imported from Caen in France into some of the earlier buildings. Early round towers were only 35 feet tall with the flints being laid in layers or very much at random. Some of the later ones are over 50 feet in height. Ornate parapets, some in the shape of battlements, were added as and when they became fashionable, usually, I believe, in the 14th and 15th centuries.

Some writers believe that several of the round tower churches, particularly those near the coast and built before the Norman Conquest, were used as observation or look-out towers to watch for invaders and in some cases, as a place of refuge. Most of the original windows were very small and believed to be partly for defensive purpose. There was a fear of invasion from the Danes and the Northmen and it is said that the litany once read, "From the fury of the Northmen, good Lord deliver us".

I am not a historian or a student of medieval architecture, but from visits to the churches, particularly the older unspoiled ones, one gains a great feeling of age and serenity. When you realise that maybe 30, 35 or even 40 generations have previously worshipped in the church in the same spot where you are standing, it is very humbling. It is also rather humbling to think of the large number of babies who will have been christened in the beautiful Norman fonts that grace many of these churches in North Norfolk. Please do not think I am being critical of the churches that have been modernised, some have been beautifully done and many, of course, have needed extensive work or they would not have survived until today.

Why do I call this book "Hidden Treasures of North Norfolk"? Many people trail through north Norfolk and maybe never, or certainly rarely, see a round tower church. There are many cases where the churches are well hidden—down narrow, very narrow in places, country lanes. Some are hidden outside the original villages they served—the villages possibly having been moved at the time of the Black Death and the churches are all that remain of the old village, a new village having grown up a short distance away. There are also one or two churches in fields and in farmyards and in fact one or two I have never even been able to find in other parts of Norfolk!

The majority of the churches are open to the public but sensibly with church silverware removed. However several are understandably, but sadly, closed. Most detailed where you could find a key, but to a stranger in the area this was occasionally almost as difficult as finding the church itself. Some churches provide small booklets that may be purchased for a nominal amount, detailing a brief history of the church. Many of these booklets are written by Richard Butler-Stoney and are extremely interesting and useful, particularly on one's first visit.

We read often of 'man's many pilgrimages' to holy places abroad and to the cathedrals and abbeys in this country. Often however, we overlook the numerous smaller, yet older, beautiful historic churches that proliferate the various areas of Norfolk and are well worthy of our pilgrimages or visits.

Suggested Tours

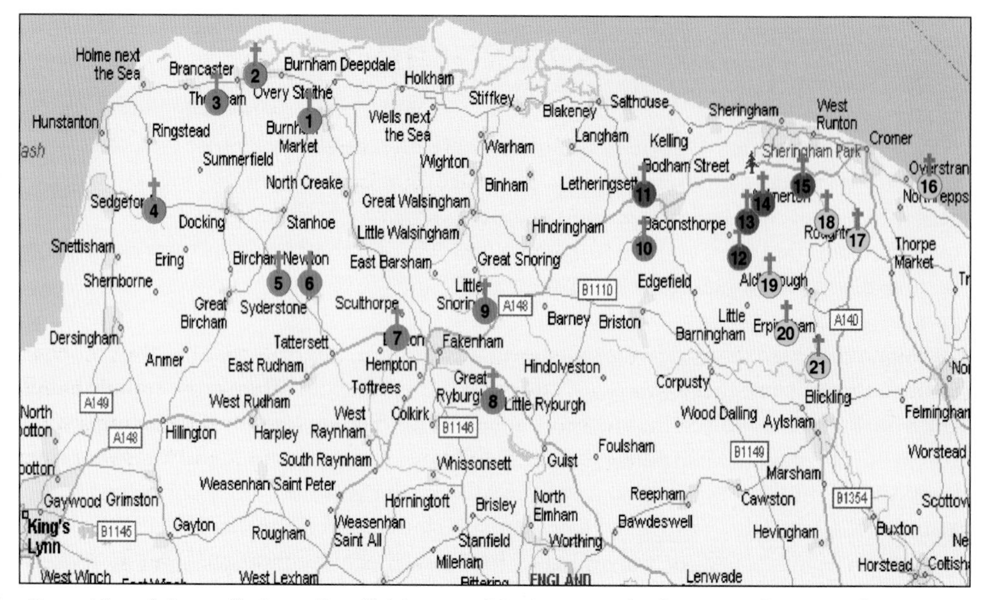

For ease of reference I have grouped the churches into four 'little tours' each starting from a slightly different base, none of which are too far apart. Before each tour, brief route details are provided to help as far as possible in reaching the locations. I would however suggest that a good road map of north Norfolk would be very useful as some of the narrow country roads, or lanes, are sometimes difficult to follow.

Tour A (from Wells next the Sea)
Burnham Norton — St. Margaret's
Burnham Deepdale — St. Mary's
Titchwell — St. Mary the Virgin
Sedgeford — St. Mary's
Barmer — All Saints

Tour C (from Holt)
Letheringsett — St. Andrew's
Matlaske — St. Peter's
Bessingham — St. Andrew's
Gresham — All Saints
Aylmerton — St. John the Baptist

Tour B (from Fakenham)
Syderstone — St. Mary's
Shereford — St. Nicholas
Great Ryburgh — St. Andrew's
Little Snoring — St. Andrew's
Stody — St. Mary's

Tour D (from Cromer)
Sidestrand — St. Michael and All Angels
Roughton — St. Mary the Virgin
Sustead — St. Peter and St. Paul
Wickmere — St. Andrew's
Thwaite — All Saints
Ingworth — St. Lawrence

N.B. 1 Churches in Tours C & D are fairly close to each other as seen from local signposts.
N.B. 2 Some of the roads in Tours, B C and D are very narrow.

Tour A commencing from Wells-next-the-Sea

Burnham Norton – St. Margaret's
Burnham Deepdale – St. Mary's
Titchwell – St. Mary the Virgin
Sedgeford – St. Mary's
Barmer – All Saints

Leaving Wells, take the A149 toward Hunstanton. Approximately six miles out of Wells (beyond Holkham Hall and Burnham Overy) look over to your left—at the top of the hill you will see St. Margaret's Church, Burnham Norton. This is approached by taking a small road (B1355) on the left hand side, up approximately 400 yards to the church on your right hand side.

On leaving Burnham Norton, return to the A149 bearing left for two miles towards Burnham Deepdale. St. Mary's is beside the road on the right-hand side.

Leaving Burnham Deepdale, continue on the A149 through Brancaster Staithe and Brancaster for three miles. Take a small side road to the right toward St. Mary's, Titchwell.

Leaving Titchwell, again returning to the A149, follow the road through Thornham, Holme next the Sea, by-pass Hunstanton and Heacham, and after eight miles (by the Norfolk Lavender premises) turn left on the B1454 signposted to Docking. Proceed on this road for approximately a mile reaching Sedgeford. Take the first turn to the right and first right again along Church Lane, and St. Mary's is in a valley on the left-hand side.

Return back to the B1454, continuing on through Docking towards Fakenham. Barmer is approximately nine and a half miles from Sedgeford. The old church of All Saints is set in a field on the left-hand side, approximately half a mile before the small village. It is approached by a cart track through the field. It is possible to drive on this rather bumpy track towards the church, but it is perhaps preferable to leave the car on the main road. After visiting the church return to the B1454 to join the A148 towards Fakenham, approximately five miles.

N.B. The next destination, which is detailed under Tour B, is St. Mary's Church at Syderston. This can be included in this tour by proceeding down the A148 towards Fakenham. After two miles, branch left to Syderston. The church is at the end of the village on the left hand side.

St. Margaret's of Burnham Norton

As I mentioned earlier, this church is set picturesquely on a hill overlooking the fields, marshes and sea and its coastal village. It is thought that the original village may have been much nearer the church and the Carmelite Friary, the remains of which I'll discuss briefly later. The village may have moved as the result of the Black Death in 1349–50, but other causes may be likely.

It is interesting that here is a church which generates such differing views on age and origin. Over the years, I have visited this church on several occasions and I have purchased three small booklets and also referred to W. G. Goode's and other research. Unfortunately they are inclined to disagree on actual age. Most feel that the tower and part of the church are Saxon, i.e. between 1000 AD and the Conquest, whilst one or two feel that it is later, maybe Norman because a church is not specifically referred to at Burnham Norton in the Domesday Book of 1086. I prefer to feel that parts of the church, particularly parts of the tower (except for

Figure 2

Figure 3

the addition of the 'battlements' at a later period), were built in the Saxon period, possibly early in the 11th century. Various other additions were made mainly during the Norman and early English period of possibly 13th century onwards.

This is a large beautiful church, full of character and interesting detail. Possibly because of the size of the congregation, heating problems, etc., pine screening has been erected between the arcades. Whilst some may feel that this is an unfortunate feature, I feel common sense has prevailed to give a more 'homely' feeling for the congregation. There are contrasting pillars to the arcades—13th century round pillars on the North side and octagonal 14th century on the South side.

This church has many features of note, the oldest being the rather massive font (figure 2) which, whilst not being as intricately carved as some of the fonts in the north-west Norfolk area, is, by its bold simplicity, very striking. The font standing on four rather stumpy legs (and a central drainage pillar), is surrounded by an impressive carpet made by members of the congregation in the 1990s.

Figure 4

There are two pulpits, the most distinctive being the Wine Glass Pulpit (figure 3) dating from 1450 which many consider to be one of the best of its type anywhere in the county. The pulpit, which is no longer used, was given by John and Catharine Goldale in 1450. They are portrayed on the pulpit together with four Latin Doctors, or Saints of the church, namely Ambrose, Gregory, Jerome and Augustine. It is said that John Goldale may not have been as perfect a man as the pulpit may suggest, for a few years earlier he and two others were 'arrested' for stealing oysters! There is another pulpit in the church, which is used regularly. It is fairly plain and is said to have been made in Victorian times from Jacobean panelling found in the church.

The Rood Screen was given in 1458 by William and Johanne Groom. The panels are said to include paintings of saints, and one of the donors. Unfortunately the panels were defaced at the time of the Reformation but the screen has been restored in more recent times.

Figure 5

Figure 6

There are various wall paintings within the church including two Royal Arms, one dedicated to William III (figure 4) on which the date of 1697 is boldly shown. The other Arms are in respect of George IV, 1818–1830, (figure 5). Incidentally, when these Arms were restored in 1962 it was discovered they had been painted over the Arms of Charles I.

Near the North Door is a recess which was a Wafer Oven, possibly used for baking wafers for the Mass. The organ is of a fairly recent origin, having been built in 1985 by Roger Pulham of Charsfield in Suffolk.

There is a striking east window (figure 6) but it is fairly modern and glazed in the late 1920s. It depicts two St. Margaret's—St. Margaret of Antioch and St. Margaret, Queen of Scotland who died in 1093.

Figure 7

Carmelite Friary

This Friary which is a short distance away is actually nearer Burnham Market than Burnham Norton. The Friary was founded in 1241 by Sir William de Calthorpe and Sir Roger de Hemenshale. The remains of the gatehouse (figure 7) can still be seen with its 14th century decoration, a short distance from the church. The gatehouse is in very good condition and is two and a half storeys in height with a ground floor having an excellent vaulted ceiling. The remainder of the rooms are at the rear of the gatehouse. This Friary is thought to have been the first Carmelite Friary established in Norfolk.

St. Mary's of Burnham Deepdale

This church is set beside the main coastal road (A149) road between Wells next the Sea and Hunstanton, approximately eight miles from Wells.

Whilst the church has a particular beauty of its own, it is notable for three main features: the Anglo Saxon round tower, the magnificent Norman font and its collection of medieval glass.

The round tower and the west wall are believed to be Saxon, possibly over 950 years old. The photograph (figure 2) shows the various layers of flint stone and the belfry window openings covered with trellis. The roof to the tower was thought at one time to have been tiled, but is now lead capped. The lower part of the tower is a few inches thicker than the remainder of the tower and does not appear to be of early Saxon origin. It has possibly been extensively repaired or restored at some later period.

Figure 2

Various additions to the church took place in Norman times (i.e. the North doorway), early

Figure 3

English and at later periods. Various restorations to the building occurred during the late 18th and during the 19th centuries. At one time the church was said to have become rather dilapidated and to have the aspect of 'a gloomy moss-covered cavern'. Luckily this is much changed and the church is now a great credit to all who have worked on its restoration.

The Chancel arch shown in figure 4 is of the Perpendicular Period is believed to date back to the late 15th century. The modern wrought iron screen was added in the 1930s.

The Norman font (figure 5) is a magnificent example of the Norman fonts found in the North Norfolk area. Said to be made of barnack stone from Rutlandshire, it is in effect a calendar font, featuring the rural activities of each month of the year. The font has had an interesting past and in 1797 when an attempt was made to move it, it shattered into three pieces and was moved to a garden of a Rectory in Fincham where it remained for nearly 50 years. It was then returned, partially repaired and then again many years later, the restoration was done in detail, recutting and regrinding small portions, particularly the month of October, to restore it to its present glory.

The church has a rich and varied collection of Medieval glass believed to be largely 14th and 15th century. The west window of the north aisle is an excellent example of this. Behind the pulpit is a small rectangular window glazed with Medieval glass (figure 3). It shows a deep red cross within a red circle with a deep blue infill and rectangular surround. On leaving the church there are two very interesting porch windows and at the top of these are two sections known as the sun and the moon (figures 6 and 7). There are various assorted fragments within the windows and the words 'death, where is thy sting?'

Figure 4

Figure 5

Figure 6

Figure 7

St. Mary the Virgin of Titchwell

This church (also shown on the front cover) is set in idyllic situation, very close to the main coastal road and some three miles from St. Mary's Burnham Deepdale and appears to be almost a sister church with many features being very similar. It is thought there was a church in Titchwell at the end of the 11th century and that certain portions of the church, i.e. the lower section of the tower etc., were of the Saxon period. Most of the church seems to have been built, or at least certainly altered extensively after the Conquest. One of the most interesting and unusual features is the lead covered spirelet (figure 2) on the roof of the tower. This is topped with a prominent cross.

Figure 2

The early part of the church was a fairly simple rectangle in design, consisting of a tower, nave and chancel. In the 15th century, during the Perpendicular period, the Church was widened

Figure 3

slightly to its existing size. An earlier 13th century doorway was re-erected in its present position and the South porch was added. There is an interesting small stoup set in the wall at one corner of the porch. It is thought that the church was at one time thatched but that it has been replaced by a slated roof, retaining the same lines as the original thatched roof.

Further restoration took place in 1902 when many features, which had been plastered over, were uncovered. Examples of these uncovered remains are evident particularly in the south-east portion of the chancel, where there is the remains of a piscina (figure 3) which has been spoiled by the addition of a large window beside it. The Screen was also restored at this time when much of it had to be renewed.

Figure 4

Figure 5

The font (figure 4), Norman in origin which stands on a modern spiralled base, is rather large and shaped like a tub as babies were at one time fully immersed during baptism. The font is unusual and is said at one time to have been used as a water trough in a field outside the church. It was restored to its proper use and given its new base in late 19th century. There is also a rather ornate pedestal font (figure 5) which was used at the time when the Norman font was watering cattle; it now stands at the East end, near the altar. This font is stated to date back to 1798.

Figure 6

In the tower there is a west window said to be built in Victorian times but using Norman styling. Above this window is a fairly small, triangular shaped window which may possibly be original. It is believed the majority of stained glass in the church dates from late in the 19th century. In the nave the stained glass shows a series of biblical scenes with the tracery lights showing angels, crown and medieval musical instruments. An example of the glass is shown in figure 6.

Leaving the church and returning to the main road, an ancient village cross may be seen (figure 7) similar to crosses in several other Norfolk parishes. This may well have been used as a preaching or meeting place.

Figure 7

St. Mary's of Sedgeford

Figure 2

Many churches have been built on land slightly raised above the village, but this church is very unusual in that it is low down in a valley, on the edge of the village. It is an extremely large church, almost cathedral-like in its appearance. It is strange to see such a large church in a small village and possibly the village was much larger in earlier times.

The church has had many bits and pieces added to it during the years. Again this is a church where historians argue as to the date of the earlier parts of the Church. Many feel that the tower and the lower parts of the nave and chancel were pre-Conquest, possibly just over 1,000 years old, whereas other historians feel that the round tower is Norman, with an octagonal top added at the end of the 13th century. The main walls of the church are old flint with parts of carstone.

Figure 3

The nave roof was raised and the clerestory and aisles added during the mid-1400s. The supporting pillars to the arches are mainly very solid looking, round pillars, but there is one on the north side which is hexagonal. There are two matching porches both with triangular window openings (figure 3) on the south and north sides of the church. The north porch is now the main entrance. The aisles as mentioned above, were extended to provide vestries etc., on either side of the tower (figure 2). There is a transept on the southern side of the church which is believed to be 14th century Decorated period. The chancel was shortened in 1780 because it is said to have been neglected by the Dean and Chapter of Norwich Cathedral at that time and became dangerous. The east wall was then rebuilt. Up until the time of the Reformation, the Prior and the monks of Norwich Priory were responsible for the church and its repair.

Figure 4

Internally, the church at first appears to be rather plain and austere with little decoration. On further investigation it does however, have many striking features. The font (figure 4) is impressive: Norman with a square bowl of Purbeck marble set on four circular legs, and a central drainage pier which has been renewed. It has a dominant appearance, being raised on one large and three smaller steps. Near the main entrance door is a fine 16th century Venetian chest with poker-work designs on the front. The organ, situated in the transept, dates back to 1862. There is also an interesting reading desk said to have been given by the Dean and Chapter of Norwich Cathedral when the cathedral was being restored in the 1860s. Figure 5 shows a bier, still in excellent condition, which was bought by public subscription to mark the coronation of George V in 1911. This is situated quite near to the main entrance.

Figure 5

Figure 6

Most of the windows on the north side of the church are plain glass but there are stained glass windows in both the chancel and in the west end of the church. There is also a distinctive, possibly 13th century, window in the chancel on the north side. Figure 6 shows a stained glass plaque in a window on the south side of the nave, which is dedicated to a G.H. Jacob, church warden for 22 years, and his wife Elizabeth, and was presented in 1938. The actual date of the glass plaque is unknown but possibly from the 19th century. In front of the glass plaque is one of a number of plaster corbels. Others are in the south transept and also above the organ, presumably they were all in the nave roof before it was re-roofed in the 1860s.

There are several wall paintings. The oldest, on the south side of the nave, shows very faint traces of a large St. Christopher carrying the infant Jesus on his shoulder over the water. There are also frescoes painted on the walls at each end of the church believed to have been done during the late 19th century by the Rector at that time, a Reverend J.A. Ogle.

All Saints of Barmer

Certainly one of 'the hidden treasures'! A difficult church to find—set in a field alongside the B1454 from Docking to Fakenham just before the village of Barmer. The church is approached along a bumpy path through a field about 100 yards from the road.

Figure 2

This church is thought by some historians to be early-English with a Norman tower. Others however believe there is evidence that parts of the nave of this very old church, also mentioned in the Domesday Book, are in fact Saxon. The church, because of its isolated position, had been much neglected until the maintenance was taken over by the

Figure 3

Norfolk Churches Trust a few years ago. It has now been renovated and is, I believe, used for services once or twice a year.

The Domesday Book mentions Barmer as having half a church in 1086 when possibly the nave existed at this time and the tower may have been added in the Norman or very early English period. The tower, which shows two English lancet windows, is short and the top two feet were restored when fairly recent renovations were completed. The north aisle which is shown in figure 2, would appear to be 14th century with wide tracery windows at each end. The chancel, also shown in figure 2, was largely rebuilt in the late 19th century.

The south doorway is also of the early English period. Above the door, the arch is filled with a cast iron crest of the Kerslake family (figure 3). The Kerslake family were responsible for the early restorations of the church in the 19th century. The church was used for laying out and burials and it became a mausoleum for the family, who lived in Barmer Hall. There is also a memorial to the Kerslake family (figure 5) on the floor of the church, and a further wall memorial at the nearby Syderstone church.

Figure 4

The inside of the church is rather bare and shows evidence that services are only held on rare occasions. Figure 4 shows the early English, possibly 13th century arch with a modern

English font. Figure 6 shows the arch between the nave and the chancel and the early 14th century arches between the nave and the north aisle.

This beautiful little church is set in a round (or circular) churchyard, which is believed to have been the site of a very early Saxon pagan temple, before Christianity came to Norfolk in the 7th century. The church is one of several in the county that demonstrates the Christian victory over Paganism. The churchyard contains many fine trees but at the time of my first visit, was rather overgrown and had a somewhat eerie effect. Whilst there my companion developed stomach pains and I developed a severe sharp headache. Luckily, these disappeared within minutes of our leaving. Maybe the 'spirits' did not approve of our visit! At subsequent visits, we have had no 'ill effects'!

Figure 5

Figure 6

Tour B commencing from Fakenham

Syderstone – St. Mary's
Shereford – St. Nicholas
Great Ryburgh – St. Andrew's
Little Snoring – St. Andrew's
Stody – St. Mary's

If you have not visited Syderstone on Tour A, leave Fakenham on the A148 towards Kings Lynn. After approximately four and a half miles, turn right on the B1454. After a mile take a further right turning towards Syderstone. The church is at the top end of the village.

Return towards Fakenham. On nearing Fakenham turn right on the A1065 towards Swaffham. About a mile or so out of Fakenham turn right along a narrow road toward Shereford, for approximately a mile and a half. This is a very small village and the church is set on the right hand side on a corner in a narrow country lane.

Return towards Fakenham and take the Fakenham ring road and the A1067 towards Norwich. After about three miles turn right to Great Ryburgh. The church is set in the centre of the village on the left hand side.

Return towards Fakenham and take the A148 towards Cromer. After approximately a mile and a half turn left to Little Snoring. The church is in a slightly elevated position at the far end of the village on the right hand side.

Return to the A148 (towards Cromer) for approximately two and a half miles. Turn right on the B1354 towards Aylsham. After approximately two miles turn left on the B1110 through Briningham and turn right towards Stody for approximately a mile. The church is on your left hand side at the end of the village.

After leaving the church, return to the B1110 and continue towards Holt.

St. Mary's of Syderstone

This church is set at the top of the village street in a well-maintained church-yard with the church standing impressively at the highest point. This church is now quite small, in fact almost back to its original size, with tower nave and chancel. It is a church which gives a great feeling of warmth and comfort, much enhanced I feel by the turquoise blue carpeting and hangings (figure 2).

Figure 2

Some feel that the early part of the church is Norman although there appears to be evidence that it is most likely late Saxon, built mid-11th century. Some historians insist that the church was built originally in a cruciform shape with a central tower, the tower collapsing in the 12th century and the present tower built soon after, possibly in the 13th century. The south aisle was added during the Norman period and the north aisle in the 14th century. Both aisles later became in a poor condition and were demolished. The north wall shows signs of pointed arches, which are now closed off. These appear to date from early in the 14th century and would have led to the north aisle (figure 3).

Figure 3

The main doorway (figure 4) was moved from the south aisle and now forms a western doorway in the tower. This was moved when the aisles were possibly demolished in the 18th century. There is a niche over the door which contains a small animal, possibly a lion or a dog.

On entering the church through the tower, one enters the nave. It is interesting that the pillars built in Norman times, which formerly lead to the south aisle, are large round pillars and those on the northern side of the church, built in the 14th century, are octagonal. Corbels show the Arms of the Lords of the Manor and those of the patrons.

The chancel has an impressive east window (figure 5) of the 14th century Decorated period. The glass which is quite striking was, I understand, added at the end of the 1939-45 war, a rejoicing at the return of peace. The glass shows a Nativity group with a garland of angels over. The other chancel windows are of the Perpendicular period. On the north side of the chancel there is a memorial to Rector George Hall. This may have been constructed from panels of an earlier tomb.

The font is relatively modern and the choir stalls, pulpit and pews are Victorian and are the work of local craftsmen. Many will be interested by the board detailing the Rectors of Syderstone dating back to William D. Witchington in 1309.

Figure 4

Figure 5

St. Nicholas of Shereford

The village of Shereford is named in the Domesday Book under its earlier name of Sciraforda, which means 'ford over clear water'. This is a very small parish of only 842 acres and the population is correspondingly very small. This beautiful little church, in its well-kept churchyard is a great credit to all who have cared for it. The church was originally larger in that a north aisle was added in the 13th Century but was subsequently demolished. Evidence of this can be seen on the outside of the northern wall of the church.

Figure 2

There is said to be evidence of sun worshipping in the area before the days of Christianity. The Saxon tower was probably built between 950 and 1000 AD and other evidence points to much of the church being built at the same time. There are bands of conglomerate or pudding stone mixed together with flint, both in the church and in the tower walls. Two old Saxon windows can be found, one in the west side of the tower, the other in the south nave wall. Other windows were added later and are simple wide tracery windows of the 13th century and a square headed chancel window of the 14th century. The large east window, one of the first things one notices when entering the churchyard, has flowing tracery of the 14th century Decorated period.

Figure 3

The tower roof which was repaired in 1976, has an attractive shallow lead capping. There is a very interesting Norman doorway between the tower and the nave, and inside the doorway on the tower side can be seen the remains of an older Saxon doorway. This was taller than the Norman doorway which is so prominent (figure 2). An impressive iron grill or door has been fitted to the door opening.

Figure 4

Internally the church with its fairly narrow nave and high walls, really gives the feeling of an old, unspoilt church although in fact it is said to have been highly restored in the 19th century. Obviously this was done with great care and affection.

There is a fine solid looking font with a circular bowl with scallops round the base of the bowl. It is set on a bold circular shaft with four decorative demi-pillars. All is then set on a solid plinth of stone which gives it an extremely impressive appearance (figure 3). Nearby there is a tiny pew at the north west corner which is possibly the oldest carpentry in the church—this can also be seen behind the font in figure 3.

Near the tomb recess in the north wall of the chancel (figure 4) lies a very old stone coffin lid which could be of the early English period. In the chancel there is an tombstone to an Anne Reynolds, aged 10, who died in 1772. A stone headstop, which resembles the head of a nun or a monk (figure 5) can be found between two of the arches. It is thought to provide a connection to the Convent of Lewes who were patrons of the church during the 14th and 15th centuries.

Figure 5

St. Andrew's of Great Ryburgh

Again, another church where there is great debate over the dates of origin. Mr. W.J. Goode in his book 'Round Tower Churches of South-East England' considers, although not all experts agree with him, that at least the lower part of the tower i.e. the first 12 feet or so, is late Saxon. Large amounts of conglomerate and/or carstone, are found in the construction of that part of the tower. These materials are found also in parts of the nave, particularly in the north-west corner. The tower has an attractive octagonal belfry (figure 2) added in the 14th century with a plain parapet above. Between the tower and the nave is an archway (figure 3) which appears to have been modified during Norman times—the archway also houses the font. This relatively modern font is imposing particularly with the very ornate cover over. During the 14th century, the long transepts

Figure 2

Figure 3

were added on the north and south sides of the church, giving an almost cross-like or cruciform pattern or plan of the church. The church windows are from both the Decorated and Perpendicular periods.. The Victorian porch (shown in figures 1 and 2) on the south side of the church was not built until late 19th century. A doorway at the west side of the tower originally had a small porch and at that time it was used as the main entrance.

The interior of the church is very dignified and, in fact, quite unusual because of the presence of the large transepts. A screen partitions off part of the north transept to form a vestry and on this screen is listed the various Rectors, etc. Among the lists is one of the Bishops of the Diocese of East Anglia dating back to St. Felix, in AD 630. As from 673 AD the northern section of the Diocese came under the cathedral at North Elmham.

The screen for the south transept (figure 4) is a memorial to those who died in the 1914-1918 war. This has been built in a Medieval style and depicts paintings of Norfolk saints. Over the screen are the words "Think and Thank" which is most appropriate and possibly something we should all do more often.

Figure 4

The chancel is stated to have been restored in 1910 by Sir Ninian Comper. He was a famous church architect of the period and also a designer of church interiors. The impressive chancel ceiling (seen in figure 5) was also designed by Comper. Within the chancel is a Buttes monument which is very striking. The front panel of the monument is set against the wall and an empty stone coffin has been placed against its base. Thomas Butte died in 1592 and the family coat of arms are shown over the monument. Below there is an imposing slab in the floor with a huge coat of arms to the members of the great Norfolk family of Bacon who were premier Baronets of England.

Figure 5

St. Andrew's of Little Snoring

Figure 2

A village which to the outsider, like several others in Norfolk, has a very strange name. The names of both Great Snoring and Little Snoring are said to derive from the Saxon invaders of AD 450—shortly after the Romans left the country. The church is on the outskirts of the village, on slightly rising ground and separated from the village by a small stream. This church, mentioned in the Domesday Book, is unique in that it is the only round tower church in Norfolk with a detached tower. There is also a detached round tower church in Suffolk at St. Andrew's in Bramfield.

There is some confusion regarding the differing ages of the tower and of the church nearby. As seen in the photograph of the tower, (figure 2) almost definitely Saxon, the rooflines are clearly shown of the earlier church. It is believed that the old church may

Figure 3

have been demolished because of flooding from the nearby stream which most likely, was then much larger. The tower is mainly flint built with small amounts of carstone. On the east side of the tower the arch is also of carstone as can be seen in figure 2. The tower has a relatively unusual conical tiled roof dating from probably the late 17th Century.

The present church, which is set slightly north east of the church tower, appears to have been built mainly some 100-150 years after the tower although part of the material from the earlier church may have been used in the new building. The older part of the church is thought to be Norman with later additions at various periods. The south doorway consists of three arches, part being a plain Norman arch, part early English and the outer section of a slightly later period, possibly 13th/14th century. The church has a large range of window styles dating from early English, Decorated and Perpendicular and Tudor periods.

Inside the church, which is relatively plain, there are various points of interest, for example, the font (figure 3) believed to be Norman with a bold round bowl with a floral and foliage design set on a strong shaft decorated with semi-pillars on a solid round base. The mahogany pulpit is said to date from about 1780, the mahogany having been imported from Jamaica earlier that century. Above the south doorway is a unique example of the coat of arms of James II's reign and dated 1686 (figure 4). The coat of arms shows rampant lion and unicorn and various inscriptions. In the chancel there is a striking piscina in the south-east corner (figure 5)

Figure 4

Figure 5

On the south of the nave, there is a plaque that commemorates the RAF's use of the church in 1944 and 1945 when the land immediately to the north-west became a very active airfield leading up to and during the invasion of Europe. When the Officers' Mess was demolished several 'awards boards' were given to the church listing the sorties from Little Snoring and the victories and various decorations awarded (example shown inside front cover). These boards are on the west wall of the nave. Also on the west wall of the nave is a poem by S.F.Ruffel, an airman who served at RAF Little Snoring. The poem, which is well worth reading, tells of the harshness and bitterness of war and hopes for the future.

St. Mary's of Stody

The church stands on a small hill at the end of the village and is approached by narrow, winding lanes. Some historians feel that parts of the original sections of the church, i.e. parts of the nave and the chancel, which incidentally have no screen to divide them, are Saxon. Their width and thickness and also evidence of conglomerate being used in the lower portions, points to such a dating. The transepts and south porch were added in the 15th century, making this a large church for a rather small village. Although there are few houses nearby, this may be another case where the Black Death much diminished the village in the late 14th century.

Figure 2

The round tower, which is also believed to be largely Saxon, shows varying layers of different sizes of flint, sections have possibly been added at regular intervals. The belfry windows were possibly added in the mid-14th century and the battlement portion with its white napped flint added in the 15th century.

Internally, because of the high roof and the large windows, the church has a great feeling of light and airiness. The windows, mainly of the Perpendicular period in the nave, are nearly all plain glass with one or two small coloured portions. The coloured portions are believed to be mainly 15th century. The chancel windows are earlier, being of the Decorated period with various tracery. The very impressive east window (shown in figure 2), which has been recently restored, is said to be of the 13th century.

Figure 3

Figure 4

The large octagonal font (figure 3), believed to be 13th century, is of Purbeck marble with rather well-worn arches in its design. The cracked bowl, is set on a central drainage column with additional supporting pillars. This then stands on an impressive double decked stone plinth. The font, set virtually under the high tower arch, is shown in figure 4 which also details the vaulted timber roof. The pulpit, also shown in the photograph, was built in memory of a Mary Fullagar who died in 1906.

There are several black stone floor slab memorials. Figure 5 shows an unnamed memorial with a deeply cut dolphin. This memorial is said to be for a William Symonds, who died in 1689, and his wife who died several months later. There is also a memorial to a Captain

Figure 5

Charles Brittiff, a mariner who died aged 76 in 1741, and his wife. The shield on this memorial shows three seashells.

There are several other very interesting items within the church which was restored early in the 20th century. The pulpit as mentioned above, and choir stalls were added early in this period and the pews of solid oak, a few years later. There is also a stone arch piscina in the chancel as shown in figure 6.

The detailed list of Rectors dates back to 1262.

Figure 6

Tour C commencing from Holt

Letheringsett – St. Andrew's
Matlaske – St. Peter's
Bessingham – St. Andrew's
Gresham – All Saints
Aylmerton – St. John the Baptist

Leave Holt on the A148 towards Fakenham. Just over a mile outside Holt you reach Letheringsett, passing the watermill on the left and approximately 250 yards further along the church is set back on the right hand side at the top of a small lane.

On leaving Letheringsett, return on the A148 to Holt. Leave Holt on the B1149 towards Norwich. After about three and a half miles at Edgefield Green, turn left towards Plumstead and on to Matlaske (approximately three miles from Edgefield Green).

On leaving Matlaske continue towards Bessingham approximately two miles. The church is at the far end of the village in an elevated position on the left hand side at a road junction.

Leaving Bessingham, continue on the road towards Gresham, approximately a mile and a half. On reaching Gresham, which is rather a sprawling village, the church is on the outskirts of the town on the left hand side of the road towards Aylmerton.

After leaving Gresham continue on the road towards Aylmerton for about a mile. The church is at the far end of the village in a raised position.

On leaving Aylmerton continue on towards the A148 approximately a half a mile. Turn right towards Cromer, approximately five miles.

N.B. Tours C and D are in parts very close to each other and can be mixed as required.

St. Andrew of Letheringsett

Figure 2

One of the original names of Letheringsett was Laringaseta and appears in the Domesday Book of 1086. Some feel that the round tower is early Norman and was built just after that date, but others think that the tower, except for the very top, is very late Saxon, some time between the year 1000 and the time of the Norman Conquest. The narrow slit type window openings appear to be Norman but are not stone dressed as is usual. The upper windows with plain tracing, were added later. C.L.S. Linnell, writing in the Parish Guide in the 1950s also mentions traces of circular windows that have been bricked up high in the tower walls.

With regard to the rest of the building, it is probable that a church was built at the time of the tower. Whilst the nave and chancel's basic dimensions are virtually Saxon, the present

Figure 3

church has been built after that period, possibly Norman, with additions of the north and south aisles in the 13th century. The south doorway may also have been built at this time but the porch was added in 1875. This is a church which has been repaired and renovated particularly during the Victorian era and in the 1950s and 1970s and has always been kept in excellent condition.

The church is set in a lovely position, laid back from the A148 road, from Holt to Fakenham, only a mile or so from Holt itself. This, like many other parishes in Norfolk, was decimated possibly by the Black Death during the 14th century. There are many lovely houses nearby, some of which have provided the benefactors to keep this church in the excellent condition it is today. Within the church, which is very attractive, are memorials to some of the benefactors, particularly to the Worsley family and also to the Cozens-Hardy family.

The inside of the impressive roof (figure 2) is relatively modern and is continuous over the nave and the chancel. At the base of the timber roof supports are beautifully carved corbels or figures in both timber and stone (figures 3 and 4).

Figure 4

Figure 5

The 19th century Italian candelabra are also very striking. Also within the church is a Purbeck marble font (figure 5), stated to be 13th century with a pointed arch design. This is said to be similar to several other fonts in churches in the close vicinity. Another interesting feature is an 18th century barrel organ. This was originally in another Norfolk church then in a private house, and installed in St. Andrews in 1956. There is also a lovely 17th century Communion Table which came to St. Andrews in 1957.

Of the windows, those in the nave are mainly Perpendicular and in the chancel of the more attractive Decorated period. Parts of the glass in the chancel is stated to be 15th century. The east window over the altar is shown in figure 6.

Figure 6

Within the churchyard there is a tombstone to a local blacksmith, horologist and inventor who died in 1852, named Johnson Jex. There is also a head and a framed epitaph within the church. Jex lived and worked close by for over 50 years. Various watches, lathes, tools and other objects made by him are in the Castle Museum in Norwich.

St. Peter's of Matlaske

Figure 2

Again, differences of opinion exist about the age of this church. Many feel it is early Norman, but there is also much evidence that parts of the tower and the west wall may be Saxon. An unusual feature of the tower is that, up to a height of 15 feet or so, the walls are very thick and then they reduce to an upper circular section (figure 1). Above this there is an octagonal belfry which was added in the 14th century. The church is narrow and there is no chancel, the chancel walls having fallen during a service in 1726. Luckily the walls fell outward and no one was injured. The south aisle was added in the 14th century. A very interesting and prominent tower arch (figure 2) between the tower and the nave is very tall, over 14 feet. This appears to have been re-faced in recent years. Over the arch is a hatchment to the Gunton family who formerly lived in Matlaske Hall which was demolished over 50 years ago.

Figure 3

The font (figure 3) is fairly simple and plain but still very attractive. This is believed to be 15th century in origin. The decorative wooden font cover also is believed to be of a similar period.

The Royal Arms, a fairly common feature in these churches, are of George III and was beautifully restored by a local artist in 1969 (figure 4).

There are eight corbel heads supporting the nave roof. These could be portraits of those who built the church, they could be medieval characters, or could represent different moods. Examples are shown in figures 5 and 6.

A very old 14th century chest can be found at the base of the tower. It is said to have contained parish registers from the 16th century which are now safely stored in Norwich. Figure 7 shows the chest together with an old funeral bier.

This is a very attractive little church with a feeling of warmth and calmness heightened, in my opinion, by the turquoise blue carpeting and the beautifully maintained five hundred year old pews. It is all very simplistic but impressive. There are many other

Figure 4

Figure 5

Figure 6

interesting features—the piscina in the south aisle; the framed remembrance to the RAF and Fleet Air Arm Squadrons who flew from RAF Matlaske during the Second World War. There is also a wall memorial (figure 9) to a Christopher Dixon who died in 1727 aged 91—a great age nearly 300 years ago.

Figure 7

St. Andrew's of Bessingham

Figure 2

This old church sits high up on a corner at the end of the village. The church is very attractive and certainly very old. The tower is said to be one of the earliest in any of the round tower churches in the county, possibly built mid-10th century. The tower as shown clearly in figure 2, has been built in sections of 12 feet or so, mainly of carstone or gingerbread stone, as it is known in parts of west Norfolk, and flint. The west end of the nave wall near the porch (also shown in figure 2), is of a similar construction. The tower is topped with a parapet of white flints and brick. Near the top of the tower there are four sets of twin light Saxon belfry windows. Below these windows are four round headed windows that are partly bricked up. Lower down on the west side is a rectangular window capped with large flints (figure 3). The church walls have been largely rebuilt with a few Saxon portions remaining

Figure 3

Figure 4

Figure 5

as mentioned above. The church was also heavily restored in the 19th century and the tower in 1986.

There is an early round-headed arch between the tower and the nave (figure 4) which also shows an upper doorway, possibly Saxon, which would have given access to a room in the tower at a higher level.

Internally the church is very plain. There is however, an attractive 15th century pulpit and a stone font (figure 5) possibly from the same period. The windows are mainly Perpendicular style with a window in the east wall of the chancel being decorated in 20th century glass, showing Christ crowned in glory and surrounded by angels (figure 7).

There are numerous memorials to various members of the Spurrell family, formerly of Bessingham Manor, dating from early 19th century or before, up to a memorial to a Lieutenant Colonel Robert Spurrell who died in 1929 following injuries received in the

Figure 6

First World War (figure 6). This memorial also refers to the window in the east wall of the chancel mentioned earlier in figure 7. Near the memorial to Lieutenant Colonel Spurrell on the north wall of the nave is a piscina.

Figure 7

All Saints of Gresham

A beautiful church set on a slight slope on the edge of the village, some three miles south of the A148. It is rather confusing to some that the village is a few miles away from the famous Gresham School, which is on the outskirts of Holt.

Figure 2

Whilst it is very difficult to date, it appears that the lower part of the tower may have been built around about the time of the Conquest, either a little before or a little after. In recent years, maybe late 19th century, the tower was renovated and given the fairly usual battlement-type parapet.It appears that the west wall of the church, which has many sections of conglomerate stone, may have been built at the same time as part of the tower but various alterations have been made. The church was enlarged and slightly widened, possibly in the 13th and 14th

Figure 3

centuries and part of the original conglomerate stone was re-used in the north and south nave walls. The chancel also appears to have been added during this period. The church has an impressive two storey porch (figure 2) where the gable end is capped by a cross with a 'ring of glory'. This porch provides an imposing entrance to the church.

One of the more attractive features internally, is the fine 15th century seven-sacrament font which is said to be one of the best in the country. The font is in excellent condition, having been protected by plaster for many years. The eight-sided font (figure 3, detail in figure 4) has many interesting scenes, including the Baptism of Christ, Holy Communion, Baptism of children, Holy Matrimony and the Ordination.

Figure 4

Figure 5

There are many memorials in the chancel, the earliest being to a Reverend Robert Smith dated 1658. There are six memorials to the Spurgin family including the Reverend John Spurgin who died in 1893. There are also six memorials to the Batt family, who formerly lived in Gresham Hall. One of the most interesting is to three army officers, the three younger sons of the family, who died during the 1939-45 world war, two of them within a few days of each other, in August 1944 (figure 5). For one family to lose three sons in such short a period emphasises the sadness and tragedy of war.

In the north-west corner of the nave is a small pipe organ dated 1867 and given to the church in 1893. The stained glass is mainly Victorian including figure 6 on the east wall of the chancel. The window (see back cover) on the south wall of the nave is said to be late 19th century.

Figure 6

The village sign opposite the church shows the Arms of the Gresham family, the Paston family and of Thomas Chaucer, the son of Geoffrey Chaucer, author of Canterbury Tales, and his wife. Below is shown Gresham Castle, a windmill and a watermill. The large grasshopper above was the emblem of the Gresham family.

St. John the Baptist of Aylmerton

Figure 2

A tall imposing church set on a hill beside the road leaving the village toward the A148. The church is some 200 feet above sea level and only two miles or so from the coast. Maybe because of its nearness to the sea, it could have been regarded as an early defence tower, but it was really built too late to fit that description.

Some believe there is evidence of a Saxon church on this site and the original may have been of timber. Whilst much of the existing church is now believed to have been built after the Conquest and during the Norman period, it is thought that the small southern

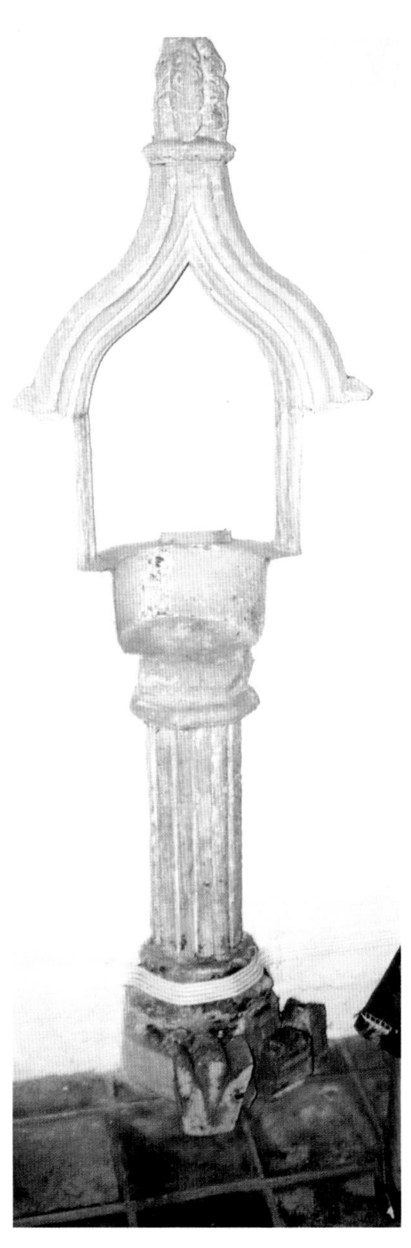

Figure 3

Figure 4

Figure 5

doorway in the tower and maybe part of the lower tower, were possibly of Saxon origin. The upper part of the tower was rebuilt in its original design in 1912. At this time the south doorway in the tower, which had been blocked for many years, was re-opened.

Walking up the slope to the church, one is first impressed by a fine two storey south doorway porch which was built possibly in the late 14th century. The chancel was rebuilt slightly earlier than the south doorway in mid-14th century. The impressive piscina and

Figure 6

Figure 7

sedilia (figure 2) were added at that time. There is also a small ornate piscina on the north wall of the nave which is believed to have been built at a later date (figure 3).

Many alterations and restorations have taken place over the years and it is difficult to ascertain the actual date of origin. The church is relatively large and would appear to have been even larger. Figure 4 shows the remains of a chapel on the north side of the nave. This was built possibly early in the 15th century and demolished during the 16th. During the 15th century various other alterations were carried out including heightening and re-roofing the nave. Further restoration took place on several occasions during the 19th century.

Internally the most impressive item is the Communion table (figure 6) of 1876. Various other items including font (figure 5), pews, organ, etc., are stated to be of the Victorian period. The 15th century rood screen has been considerably altered with various portions, including the loft, removed. Figure 7 shows this together with the arch between the nave and the chancel. Above the pulpit can be seen a bricked up opening which formerly led to the screen loft.

Figure 8 shows the old parish boundary cross about a mile from Aylmerton on the road from Gresham. This is said to date late 14th century.

Figure 8

Tour D commencing from Cromer

Sidestrand – St. Michael and All Angel's
Roughton – St. Mary the Virgin
Sustead – St. Peter and St. Paul
Wickmere – St. Andrew's
Thwaite – All Saints
Ingworth – St. Lawrence

Leave Cromer on the B1159 toward Mundesly. Pass through Overstrand and approximately four miles from Cromer, Sidestrand church is on the left-hand side, close to the road. Parking is fairly difficult as it is a busy road.

Leave Sidestrand and return to Cromer on the B1159. Just before entering Cromer turn left on the A149 towards North Walsham and Norwich. Approximately two and a half miles outside Cromer bear right onto the A140 (Norwich road). Roughton is approximately one and a half miles further on. Pass through the centre of the village and the church is in an elevated position on the left-hand side and is approached along a lane.

On leaving the church return through the village and bear left on the B1436. After approximately one mile take a left (unnumbered) road towards Metton and Sustead. The church is on the outskirts on the far side of Sustead.

Back to the country road leading south toward Thurgarten and on towards Wickmere on the right. Before you reach Wickmere, Wickmere church is set in an open position, approximately a mile from the village along a country lane. Incidentally, the key for this church can be obtained from a country house down a lane adjacent to the church.

Leaving Wickmere follow country lanes towards Earpingham on to Thwaite which lies to the west of the main A140 between Norwich and Cromer about five miles north east of Aylsham. The church is on the right-hand side of the road.

Continue on down this road to the A140 turn right towards Aylsham. At approximately three miles turn right to Ingworth. Ingworth church is set at a road junction in a slightly elevated position near the village sign on the left hand side of the road.

On leaving Ingworth, one can either return to Cromer on the A140/A149. If one wishes to go to Norwich, go through Aylsham and on the A140 south.

N.B. Tours C and D are in parts very close to each other and can be mixed as required.

St. Michael's and All Angels of Sidestrand

Figure 2

This church has an amazing story. Way back in the 1870s it was realised that the cliff on which it stood was crumbling badly and there was a very high risk of the church falling into the sea. The church, except for the tower, was moved in 1881, stone by stone, and rebuilt as near as possible as it had been before, some one third of a mile inland. The tower, a rebuild of the original, which was thought to be Saxon or early Norman, had been left where it was and fell into the sea when it finally collapsed in March 1916. The present building was erected from funds set up by Sir Samuel Hoare and colleagues. The actual building reconstruction was carried out by a North Walsham firm, Cornish and Gaymer and the new building was consecrated on Michaelmas Day 1881. The total cost of the removal and rebuilding was £2,254.2s.3d—today this would possibly cost several million!

The original church, which is said to be mainly 15th century, consists of a wide nave, chancel and south porch with the tower added at the time of rebuilding. A north vestry was added in 1907.

Internally, the font (figure 2) is believed to be 15th century with a wooden carved font cover dated 1930. The font is situated at the base of the tower and near it, fixed to the wall, are two stone coffin covers which come from the original church yard. These are believed to be 13th century or earlier.

The nave is timber panelled. The panelling was erected originally in 1936 and acts as a memorial to many departed members of the congregation. On the north side of the nave is the organ. This was earlier based in a Norwich church. Also on the north wall is a memorial to the dead from the two World Wars. This is ornately decorated with a figure of St. Michael (figure 3).

Figure 3

Figure 4

In the south wall of the nave is a piscina (figure 4) and a stone cross memorial to a William atte Wode dating early 15th century. The hanging rood screen is a memorial to Sir Samuel Hoare who died in 1915. It was made by a Belgian refugee, an English nun and a London craftsman.

The chancel was panelled earlier than the nave in 1911. The east window was erected in memory of John Gurney Hoare and his wife in the 1880s. Below this is an impressive reredos which tops the communion table (figure 5). The reredos beautifully depicts the Last Supper.

On entering the church yard it is worth looking at the grave stones on your left hand side that are placed against the boundary wall (to the road). These

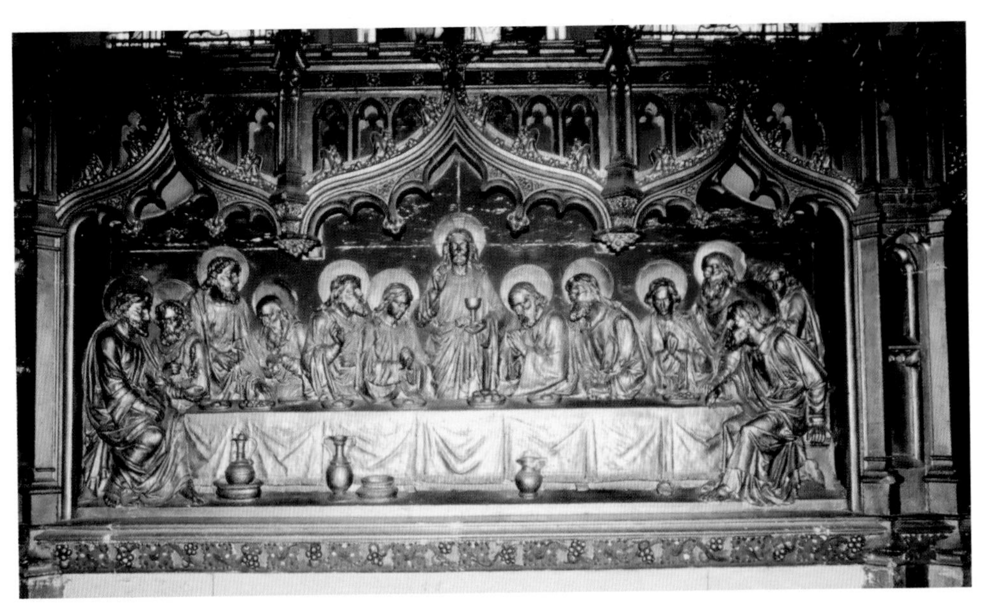

Figure 5

(figure 6) are from the graveyard of the old church and were moved here at the time of the rebuilding.

The churchyard of the old church gained fame back in the 1860s when Clement Scott, who was a renowned drama critic at the Daily Telegraph, called the churchyard a 'garden of sleep' and it also became known as 'Poppyland'.

Figure 6

St. Mary the Virgin of Roughton

This is another parish that was mentioned in the Domesday Book under various names of Ruftana, Roftuna and Rustuna. The parish underwent various name changes over the centuries until it was spelt Rowghtonn in the reign of Elizabeth I. Earlier 17th century records show that the church was originally named All Saints but it is now dedicated to St. Mary the Virgin

This impressive church is on slightly elevated land, a little way away from the village proper. It appears that this may be another case of the village possibly having moved at the time of the Black Death and, as time has progressed, the village is gradually moving back toward the church.

The tower is believed to be mainly from the late Saxon period and there are also traces of

Figure 2

Figure 3

Saxon work and materials in the west wall of the church. There have been extensions and alterations at various periods.

In figure 2 the construction of the fine round tower is clearly shown. Various layers of carstone and flint laid in herringbone style in the lower portion. Above this section are smaller flints, then larger flints. The battlements were added at a later period. The small circular windows at approximately 15 feet and triangular headed double windows at belfry level have almost definite Saxon signs.

There was an early chantry chapel on the north side of the church. Figure 3 shows the outside of the north wall which outlines the vaulted roof of the old chapel and the remains of a piscina which is still set in the wall.

Figure 4

In the 14th century many sections of the church were rebuilt and an aisle and the porch were added.

The elegant interior of the church is dominated by the octagonal piers and arches to the arcading of the nave (figure 4). It is said that the church has not been extensively altered since the

Figure 5

Figure 6

Figure 7

15th century except for restorations in the mid-19th and 20th centuries. The elegant roof timbers, the pulpit and altar are believed to be 15th century.

Figure 5 shows the tower arch with the organ pipes over. It also shows the octagonal font believed to be 14th Century, standing on a circular plinth with further supporting pillars (figure 6). The timber carved cover over is in excellent condition and very decorative.

The majority of the windows in the aisles are of the Perpendicular period and those in the chancel of the Decorated period. Figure 7 shows the window in the east wall over the altar with its reticulated tracery.

St. Peter and St. Paul of Sustead

The original parts of the church are thought to be Saxon with portions having being added or altered during the Norman, Tudor and Victorian periods.

The lower part of the tower, believed to be Saxon, is built mainly of flint mixed with sections of conglomerate or carstone. The belfry section of the tower was added during the 13th and 14th centuries with four belfry windows, although they were said to have been altered during the Victorian renovations of the late 1870s. The brick battlement at the top was added in the mid-18th century.

Figure 2

The nave shows evidence of very many alterations during the centuries and has windows from various periods. Some of the south wall windows have fragments of original medieval stained glass.

Figure 3

Figure 4

The chancel was built in the 14th century with major Victorian alterations. On the south side is a fine 14th century double piscina and a sedilia (figure 5) In the chancel there are also some fine, mainly 19th century windows, with some glass dated 1897, an example is shown in figure 6. The porch on the south side of the church was added late 14th century and restored during 19th century.

Figure 5

Figure 6

Figure 2 shows externally, the north side of the church and outlines a 14th century archway which is now blocked off. This led to a north transept which has been demolished. This archway can also be seen internally (figure 3) which also details the decorated 17th century pulpit, believed to have come from a redundant church in North Barningham.

The 15th century font (figure 4) shows carved armorial shields on each of the sides or faces of the bowl. Some of these shields are said to depict well known local families.

St. Andrew of Wickmere

This is a large almost isolated church set in a commanding position in open fields with very few houses nearby. The actual village is about a mile away. This may be yet another case where the village moved at the time of the Black Death.

Like so many round towered churches, there is argument about the date or dates of origin. The lower part of the tower and part of the west wall, as can be seen in the main picture, contain a large amount of carstone or conglomerate and various layers of flint, the building materials much used by the Saxons. The church was

Figure 2

Figure 3

very narrow originally with the aisles, both north and south being added during the 14th/15th century. The windows and also those of the chancel, are of the Decorated period and the windows of the white flint clerestory are very striking, being alternatively 'two lights' and 'almost diamond like' in style.

A very small window in the tower at about 20 feet or so (figure 2) appears to be of a very early period. The battlement portion of the tower added at a later date, is also of white flint.

On entering the church one first notices the ironwork (believed to be 14th century) on the inside of the door. Backing on to the west wall there is an ornate stone war memorial depicting an angel holding a scroll of honour. Nearby is a font decorated with shields and roses (figure 3)

On the north wall of the nave there are some early medieval pews or benches (figure 4). The most impressive tomb chest with robed figure and angels is that of the fifth Earl of Orford, Baron Walpole, who died in 1931 (figure 5). The first Earl was Sir Robert Walpole, the first Prime Minister of England of the modern era in the early mid-18th century. The church has strong connections with the Walpole family who adopted St. Andrew's Wickmere, when their own church St. Margaret's, Wolterton, became derelict some 300 years or so ago.

There are memorials and hatchments (example in figure 9) to the Walpole family in the chancel and nave. A portion of the graveyard has also been dedicated to the Walpole family. Several other memorials can be found in the nave. One is to a Henry Spellman who died in 1765 in Bengal having distinguished himself as a soldier.

The impressive modern pulpit has on its face 15th century panels, which are shown in figure 6. Behind the pulpit is the beautiful 15th century screen which still faintly shows some of the early paintings.

Figure 4

Figure 5

Figure 6

Within the chancel is a striking piscina with a three seat sedilia adjoining (figure 7). Also at the entrance to the chancel is a reading desk with a beautiful small medieval carving of a minstrel (figure 8).

The chancel of St. Andrews is said to be a 'weeping chancel' as there is a slight displacement to the south compared with the angle of the nave. This is quite common in medieval churches. There are various theories which relate to symbolism; orientation; the work of the devil; or to the crucifixion. The most probable conclusion mentioned in T.D. Mortlock and C.V. Roberts Guide to Norfolk Churches' is quite simply "that mathematical accuracy was not the forte of the medieval masons and that chancels being 'out of true' with the nave was straightforwardly a result of ground plan inaccuracy or expediency"!

Figure 7

Figure 8

Figure 9

All Saints of Thwaite

The parish of Thwaite appears in the Domesday book under the name of Tuit and it seems that a church has been in this location since 1035 or earlier.

Most historians feel that the tower is Saxon although others lean more towards the idea of it being early Norman, possibly of the Saxo-Norman period. The tower was highly restored in the late 19th century following gale damage and received a new surface of flints laid in regular courses to strengthen the structure. The belfry openings were made when the tower was heightened and these double openings are believed to be 13th century. The part-brick battlement was added later, possibly at the time of the restoration.

Figure 2

The remainder of the church consists of nave, (believed to be Saxon) chancel, south aisle and south porch. Various repairs and restorations have been carried out largely during the Victorian period with other major repair works in the 1980s. A Sunday School was added on the north side of the chancel mid-19th century.

Within the nave the most striking feature is the beautiful yet simple Jacobean pulpit dated 1624 (the date is shown in figure 2). The screen, the top of which was sawn off at the time of the Reformation, still shows fine medieval carpentry (shown at the side of the pulpit in figure 2). The pulpit was restored in

Figure 3

1890 and at the same time extra pews were added in the nave. Figure 3 shows the nave and south aisle, the old front box pew at the front of the nave with other older pews behind. The newer pews which were added in 1890 are shown on the right hand side. In the photograph one can also see at the back of the church, the tower arch with a peculiar semi-circular opening over.

Figure 4

Figure 5

Figure 6

There is a fairly simple and plain stone font. On the floor of the nave near the screen are several interesting stone floor memorials. One is in memory of a P.D. who died in March 1737 at the age of 12. Beside this is an undated slab faintly depicting possibly, a man and his wife with two indistinct shields above (figure 4).

In the chancel, is a brass of John Puttock and his wife (figure 5). John Puttock built the south aisle in 1442 and is buried there. In the chancel there is also a wall monument to a Reverend Theophilus Browne who was a Rector at the church and died in 1733. The monument is also in memory of his wife and his mother (figure 6).

There are several attractive stained glass windows in the church, a fine example being the window behind the pulpit (figure 7) which shows two finely clad ladies depicting Faith and Charity.

Figure 7

St. Lawrence of Ingworth

This lovely little church, roofed with Norfolk reed thatch, is said to have been in a state of dilapidation in the late 19th century. The building was greatly restored but retained its old charm with the old wooden pews, some box, remaining.

Figure 2

It is thought that the church was mainly constructed at about the time of the Norman Conquest although there are a few signs of Saxon remains. The tower (figure 1) collapsed in 1822 and only a small stump about 15–20 feet tall, remains. The tower remains are also roofed with thatch. There is a Roman

Figure 3

Figure 4

style arch between the tower and the nave. The original church was rectangular, the chancel was added in the 13th century and the south aisle and porch were added in the 14th and 15th centuries.

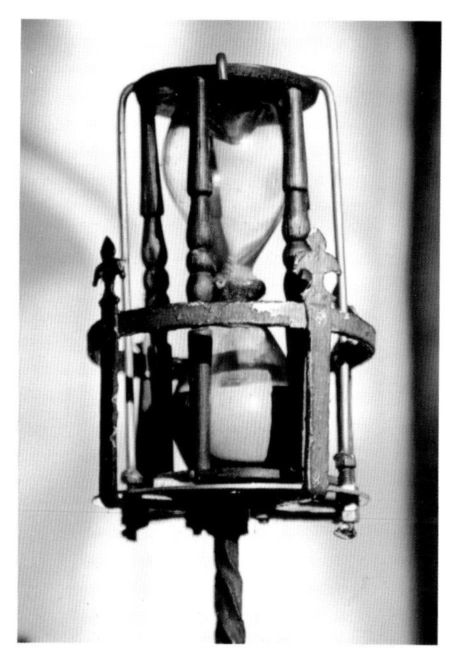

Figure 5

Figure 6

Like many of the old Norfolk churches, the chancel was separated from nave by a rood screen (figure 2). This one has been largely painted over but still shows a few remains of original colour. The upper part of the

Figure 7

Figure 8

screen and loft was destroyed at the time of the Reformation in the 16th century.

Figure 2 also shows some of the box pews with the pulpit in the background. The pulpit (figure 4) is extremely interesting. It was originally a three-decker built in the 17th century. The sermon was usually delivered from the top level. Unfortunately only one level now remains but this is still built of the original timbers. An original hour glass also remains beside the pulpit (figure 5). This used to give clergyman and congregation a good check on the length of their sermons, and possibly still does so.

The octagonal font on an octagonal pillar and stone base (figure 3), believed to be 14th or 15th century, was much damaged at the time of the Reformation. Only one of the carvings on the eight panels remain, the other seven were removed to delete any indication of decoration representing the Saints.

Another interesting feature is the very fine Arms of William III and Mary (figure 6) on the west wall of the nave. This was added before the end of the 17th century and is believed to be one of the best in the area.

There is very little stained glass remaining in the church, the main piece being the panel in the east window (figure 7).

There is a piscina in the chancel and a small stoup in the corner of the porch (figure 8).

Domesday Book References

The Domesday Book is divided into two sections: Great Domesday and Little Domesday and all the information regarding Norfolk is to be found in the Little Domesday section.

For interest I have listed below the names of the towns or villages where the churches on the previous pages are located and given their old names as at 1086. At the end I have added some notes giving my own opinion on some of the information I have obtained. Experts in these matters may not have reached the same conclusions.

Burnham Norton – (Sutton, Ulph or Westgate) – Burnaham; Burneham
Burnham Deepdale – Depedala
Titchwell – Fliceswella; Tigeswella
Sedgeford – Secesforda; Sexforda
Barmer – Benemara
Syderstone – Cidesterna; Scidesterna; Scisterna
Shereford – Sciraforda
Great Ryburgh – Reieborh; Reienburh
Little Snoring – Esnaringa; Snaringa; Snaringes
Stody – Estodeia; Stodeia
Letheringsett – Laringaseta; Laringesere; Leringaseta
Matlaske – Matelasc; Matingeles
Bessingham – Basingeham
Gresham – Gersam; Gressam
Aylmerton – Almartune; Almertuna
Sidestrand – Sistran
Roughton – Roftuna; Ruftuna; Rustuna
Sustead – Surstede
Wickmere – Wicmara; Wic Mera
Thwaite – Tuit
Ingworth – Ingewrda; Ingewurda

Notes

The Domesday Book was initially known as 'The King's Book' or 'The Great Book of Winchester' where the early royal treasury was based.

From my initial searches, the Domesday Book shows only two churches in the area covered by this book, i.e. Little Snoring and Thwaite. Barmer is also shown with half a church—possibly the church was in course of building.

I find it difficult to understand that these are the only three churches detailed as Bessingham is regarded by many historians to be one of the oldest round towered churches in the area and to date from anytime from 950 AD. Incidentally, another church at East Lexham (not included in this book) is thought to date from 850AD and still not mentioned in the Domesday Book.

It is possible that the references to churches in the Domesday Book may not be fully complete as from historic records it is said the computation of the book was completed very quickly and possibly mistakes or omissions occurred quite innocently. The book was commissioned at Christmas 1085 and completed in 1086–7 which must have been a mammoth job in view of the communications at that time. It appears the main purpose of the book was to produce a record of the returns and the resources of the land for the King's Treasury. It also shows how the parts of the country covered by the Domesday Book were split between what was owned by the King and the various Lords, Bishops and landowners who had been granted land, estates and property.

It is said that the Domesday Book was virtually out of date as soon as it had been compiled because property and land had changed hands.

Glossary

This book is written in an endeavour to raise interest in these churches and I have tried to keep the various details fairly simple but these additional notes maybe of assistance.

Aisle
These are extensions to the north and south sides of the nave.

Architectural Styles (approximate dates)

Saxon –	*7th Century to 1066*
Norman –	*1066 to approximately 1200*
Transititional –	*A period between Norman and Early English periods from approximately 1150 to 1200*
Early English –	*1200 to approximately 1300 including lancet and early tracery styles*
Decorated –	*1300 to approximation 1350 includes 'Y' tracery and reticulated style*
Perpendicular –	*From approximately 1400. This includes the Tudor styling and a Jacobean period of 1603 to 1625 during the reign of James I.*
Gothic –	*Covers an 'overall' period from approximately 1200 to 1500*

Bier
A moveable frame on which a coffin or a corpse is carried.

Black Death
1349–50—killed 20–30% of the national population but possibly over a half of the population of Norfolk.

Carstone
Also known as gingerbread stone because of its reddish brown colour (caused by iron ore particles). Very much a north west Norfolk stone.

Chancel
Eastern part of the church, housing the main altar and usually the choir.

Clerestory
This is an upper row of windows in a large church, above the level of the aisle roofs.

Conglomerate
Also known as pudding stone. Normally a harder stone than carstone and usually contains pebbles in its structure. It was originally found in the surface soil and mainly used pre-Conquest.

Corbels
These are supports, usually stone, projecting from a wall to carry the weight of the roof timbers. These are often decorated with decorative heads.

Hatchments
The Arms of a deceased person set on a black lozenge-shaped background. These hatchments were often placed in front of the home of the deceased before burial and then transferred to the church.

Lancet
Narrow, tall, acutely arched windows.

Nave
The main body of the church.

Piscina
This is a sink or stone basin usually near the altar in pre-Reformation churches for draining water used during a mass or communion. The water being drained into the consecrated foundations of the church.

Reformation
1534 when Henry VIII broke away from the Church of Rome and established the Protestant Church of England.

Reredos
An ornamental screen covering the wall at the back of the altar.

Rood Screen
A screen used to divide the chancel from the nave in many churches. In medieval churches these were largely damaged at the time of the Reformation.

Royal Coat of Arms
These were introduced into many churches after the Reformation when Henry VIII became Supreme Head of the Church of England 1534.

Sedilia
Stone seats or set of seats in the wall of medieval churches in the chancel usually near the piscina. This is where priests sat during long services.

Stoup
Usually a small stone bowl for holy water in the porches of many early churches, the water being used for parishioners to bless themselves.

Tracery
Ornate stone ribs in the upper part of windows, also seen in circular windows.

Transept
Extensions to the north and south body of the church, often leaving the church with a plan shape of the cross.

Bibliography and Suggested Additional Reading

I would like to acknowledge my thanks to the authors of some of the books listed below that have helped me in my introduction to round tower churches. If you have found the subject of round tower churches interesting, I would recommend you consider reading some these additional books:

Norfolk Churches Great and Small
by C.V. Roberts and Richard Tilbrook—an excellent book with many magnificent photographs and very interesting information.

The Popular Guide to Norfolk Churches
by T.D. Mortlock and C.V. Roberts—a series of books containing detailed information on all Norfolk churches.

Round Towered Churches of South East England
by W.J. Goode—a virtual wealth of information. A great result for over 30 years endeavour.

The Round Towered Churches of Norfolk
by Dorothy Shreeve and Lyn Stillgoe—a book of wonderful illustrations and interesting information.

England's 1,000 Best Churches
by Simon Jenkins. The contents of this book have been recently featured in a Channel 4 television series. The book covers a selection of England's finest churches and includes three of the churches visited in my suggested tours.

Miscellaneous Church Booklets
by Richard Butler-Stoney and many others. These excellent small booklets or pamphlets are normally sold at each church to help visitors.

If your interest in Round Tower churches has been roused, why not consider joining the Round Tower Churches Society. Details of membership can be found in most churches.

Wine Glass Pulpit, St. Margaret's of Burnham Norton